A Construction in Space

Poems by

– PAUL H SIMMONS –

An environmentally friendly book printed and bound in England by
www.printondemand-worldwide.com

Mixed Sources
Product group from well-managed forests, and other controlled sources
www.fsc.org Cert no. TT-COC-002641
© 1996 Forest Stewardship Council
FSC

PEFC Certified
This product is from sustainably managed forests and controlled sources
www.pefc.org
PEFC
PEFC/16-33-415

This book is made entirely of chain-of-custody materials

FastPrint Publishing

www.fast-print.net/store.php

A Construction in Space

A catalogue record for this book is available from the British Library

ISBN 978-178035-635-8

First published 2013 by
FASTPRINT PUBLISHING
Peterborough, England.

For Marion

Contents

A Construction in Space

Along the western sea the roaming breakers pull with
distant breeze,
And the blue bay is blessed with light from every side,
Calling, calling with that longing of the mind.
There the ocean's craftsman casts his net,
Strumming vibrance with the white steel threads.
Coiling currents flood the fabric bare,
And spindrift shapes itself from briny air.
Inside, the western shore is captured wild,
In studios with windows on the world;
Taut with shapeliness; soft with sound;
Settled like silken sand on solid ground.
There are no fragments here; all is one strand –
No hollow, no cove, no rock; all is steel or sand;
While the sea masters the unknown land.

Assisi

Terracotta town, clinging to its hill,
Burnished by lavish autumn sun,
Home for its pilgrims still.
They crowd the streets, equipped with their regrets,
Flock the verdant square prepared for guests,
And St. Francis on his homeward trek.
They pass the souvenirs and pious charms,
Then the market with its cold meats,
clothes and fake firearms.
Santa Chiara glows pale pink in sacred air;
A dusted angel, pausing from her trade,
Divests a blessing in the shade.

And distant to the sway of temple, church and square,
Beyond the crooked passageways and smart cafés,
St. Mary of the Angels drifts in veils below,
Beyond the walls and lofty citadel.
There on the distant, dry, green plain,
Many tears of joy and grief were cried
When once this started, and one simple man died.

A double-edged sword

I will go now and set my life free;
Having and wanting are lost now,
Call it just poverty.
I will live by the natural river,
Bathe in the icy sea,
And all I had I despise now,
Call it just poverty.
The beggars can do me no wrong now,
I'm just as pure as they,
Tired and hungry, yet wholesome,
Call it sweet poverty.
Yet everywhere voices beset me,
Family, friends and home;
Nowhere is safe, all is frightful,
Begging for alms, alone.
Night is solemn and dreadful
In winter's bitter reign,
All I despised now I long for,
Alone on the windswept plain.
The beauty of death befriends me,
She entreaties me to stay;
Prosperity once allured me,
But poverty cuts both ways.

Rebirth

Something out of nothing, goodness quite unknown,
Flourishing and growing beyond our selfish home.
We can't see the outcome, we can't find the cause,
Implicit though within us the future's taken hold.
Out of every nation, from all raging seas
Comes the omnipresent to reckon with our pleas.
Those within our remit, those from far away
Will be heard and answered, though we go astray.
With the poor and humble, less the rich and proud
All will be transformed,
Like flowers from the ground.

Intimacy

Seeing every virtue on the page, every fragment, every
story grows;
All the machinations of a crowd, or to close encounters,
secrets told.
When minds turn inward to create a world, there the shy
expression freely flows, and as we improvise to
understand, two quietudes expand the written word.
Then drama thrills with animated breath, or laughter dies
to witness tragic death.
All intimate is passion clothed with life; all clothes
companions to be undermined.
And every hour some friends to lovers turn;
And every hour confessions call us on.

Cities – in the darkest hour

Should cities talk they'd cry aloud;
Impassive walls of grand repute
Implore the people to be good –
But in between these bonds of stone
The ties of family and state
Find new recourse to kill and hate.
And many captives set within,
Their cries undone by civic haste,
Await their sentence quietly then;
They pine and die and waste.
The towers and bells of cityscape
Should take to heart the awful strife
Within the walls they brought to life;
And river, gently as it flows,
Incorporates a deadly flood,
A torrent there of tears and blood.

Lunar Nights

Languid incorruptibility melts through the air,
Embracing the land with its milky glow,
Torching the stubbled ground,
And leaving the fugitive lanced through his soul.

A barn owl quarters the pasture below,
Ranging across its domain,
Dominion of pallor and clouded light –
Etching its presence on our formless sight.

Creatures huddle, dappled in dew, touched by silver,
Wrapped like treasure. All is soft and blanched
And pristine clean – save for those running, displaced
From their past, under the insistence of the moon.

Those crying sadly as they run
Are caught by the moon as the clamorous sun;
While some lie in wonder, some welcome the new,
For lunar nights shine on the reticent too.

The empire of nails

Clasping the tenderness of wood,
The humble nail remains misunderstood.
Admit it must be driven, with force to take effect,
And without a bond it's broken, without a point, effete.
But its army is ubiquitous, it's there from shore to shore;
What house could stand without it, what tree would
  flinch no more?
They found a use for every nail and fixed it to the cross:
Uncover there its weakness; it can't redeem the cost.
And what is more its maker can cause its work to fail:
The tower as a spectacle,
In shards of language fell;
Voices overpowered it –
An empire made in hell.

Civilization

Under the Bridge of Sighs,
Across the flooded backs
The lawless waters rise.
We search but cannot find our tracks,
Debate but every word fights back;
Incessant as the water springing forth,
Or river gently lapping at its source.

The academic landscape so runs wild;
The confluence of worldly dreams,
Imagination drowned by common themes,
And passion rooted in the dull, dead earth.

But academe and parliament and Senate House
And chapel fields and bells which toll for peace
Are surely our defence against nature's influence.
The waters lap at history's door, but evermore
The intellect and culture wrap our shores.

Permafrost

Living here is to live quietly;
Living here is to die slowly.
Within this otherworld of permafrost and snow,
The future barely beckons,
The present barely grows.
Under panoplies of crystal-laden trees,
Darkness testifies to ancient times
Where little moves and nature lies confined.
Roots are bound to earth, solid earth to roots;
No winter fox or eagle presses through,
Skies are vacant as the earth below;
Deep green of ages rigid in the snow.
But tread secretly within this landscape, pristine, white,
And you may understand the sounds of life,
Confounding as it does our feeble sight.
Attend to little creaks and groans and moans;
Inner life that gently permeates, intones:
Living here is to live quietly;
Living here is to die slowly.

Consciousness

To hover on life's twisted thread,
Effortless and sinew-less,
The vision of a flower's breath
As it exhales its perfumed scent.

To find the ambergris afloat,
To dive and search the ravelled depths
With hidden lens and perfect sense,
Or sit with unconfined excess
To scour horizons for our prey,
Or doubts to quell or fear allay.

To hide within a sultry room
And penetrate its every trace
From little more than dirt and filth.

There's nothing new that's undisclosed,
Nothing old that won't be known.
For all the conscience that we hide
We share the terrain
We share the skies
We blink at the compound eye.

Clemency

There is no imprecation that cannot wither the crime,
There is no lost situation, no bitter, outrageous shame,
That won't mellow before God's mercy,
Dispelling the evil in time.
To wait for justification, to ask for clemency,
Is simply the start of a journey,
Along the path of our name.
And that name we carry and proffer
Is simple and cherished and pure,
Anointed to regain our nature
From God's temperance and care.

Faces of war and peace

The fighter flies to many foreign shores,
While pilgrims scatter petals where they walk;
And those who uphold conscience wanly fret,
Impugned in public, troubled by respect.

Among the august faces on the front,
Through the masquerade of warlike pomp,
There sneaks some predator to prey on death
Or some deserter never granted strength.

The fighter triumphs blindly in the sands,
And tears of joy erupt when he returns;
The coward soul has now a hero's breath,
The proud are vanquished, many laid to rest;

While pilgrims seek another kind of death.

Country then and now

Melancholy mixed with simplicity
Homeliness messed by infidelity;
Puritan tones of morality
Blown by the law of the gun.
Aching hearts brought low by love,
Hillbilly angels in heaven above;
Wildfire passions on the road,
Rodeo taming for a show.
Retribution on the freight train;
Sailing away to a Tex-Mex refrain;
Prison calls for a manhunt,
Swings on Virginian verandahs.
Wondering of dreams in sleep,
Lovers too difficult to keep;
But any dark hours rippling away
To the new country ballad of yesterday.

Hard Times

The globe shudders in degrees of fluid time,
It throws the sea upon us,
The sun omits to shine –
Or perhaps it never flickers
And like creatures under glass,
Fixated we endeavour,
But fixated never last.
We're destitute, in squalor,
Or trapped in fragile minds,
So how to put an aspect
To what besets mankind?
For hard times make for suffering
Which can despair or grow,
Become a fine ennoblement
Or desiccate below.
When goodness comes to recompense
It inculcates the will 'to give'
And then may raise a scholar's head
To conjugate the verb 'to live'.

Easter 2010

Look for a sign to guide you
Ask and you will see;
Predicate the present
And the future will set you free.
Enter into a mystery
That modifies all your fears
And then the presiding question
Will occupy all your years.
To understand the unknowable
Will leave much room for loss,
But beyond doubt is faithfulness
Transposed upon the cross.
The season is ready for sacrifice,
The Friday summons the soul,
The Maundy left us remembrance,
How far will we follow the call?

Once I walked in the windless night

Once I walked in the windless night,
In the furious land of forgotten dreams,
Which shift and charge
And shake their lost command.
There the oaks wear dew-soaked moss
When footfall moulds the dampened grass;
And under nightfall's constant gaze
Mere armies in the distance march.
Triumphant once, their shadows pall
The sweat-laced trail, the creeping wall
Of blackened leaves and furrowed trees,
With scent of lotus drifting through.
And in my heart the track once fresh
Now centuries on made ambient
Finds its source in restlessness,
A vital place to resonate.
So now the waking dream is past, is spent
And every tremor echoes death.

Learning

As the child reads, so we all learn,
And through the page more learning turns
The key to other worlds.
Suffice for some a little knowledge of the text,
For some a dogged physical expense.
No extrication liberates the two:
Without the one, the rest is residue.
However progress measures right or wrong,
Or compromises qualify the sum,
Only wisdom guides us wholly true,
By little paths and narrow, sheltered way
To broad expanse of bright authentic day.

Winter

December holds the land to ransom,
Quietens with its powdered snow,
And every impulse, every fancy
Can divulge but secrets now.
Nothing but the robes of winter,
White and placid as they lie,
Settling on our minds the picture
Of a darkly lucid sky.
But the sprinkling which it offers
To dispel our flagrant fears
Heralds new birth in a season,
Where cold breeds warmth
Throughout the years.

The trouble with beauty

Beauty is to eyes the place we touch,
Those eyes imperfect artists of the plan,
Those tired tourists spying grains of day,
As photographic colour seeps away.

Under stars the complex of a life explored
By every lover light years from its cause:
We visualise, we feel the pain of sight,
While all around the million miles of light.

Draw us to the beauty of the word,
A substance from beginning to the end;
For we are only shadows of a life:
Reality is beauty in the wild.

Lost Innocence

Being tempted to outgrow our past
We are the keepers of our own decay;
Once the purity we had but lost
Enriched the kindly growth of primal day.
Like an untouched fabric in the sun
Or richness in the meadows at his call
The world appeared for man so much to shun
When he espoused instead his weighty fall.
Now colours that run dry before our sight
We comprehend in nature's luscious green;
A remnant of that long-forgotten night
When innocence gave heavy birth to sin.

True innocence

Without a pre-condition, without a flaw or sin,
The happy little creature bathes in midday sun.
Submissive to its owner, yet mastered by no one,
She allows the grass to hold her, the trees to overhang.
But as she's often wonted, the garden she can shun;
Just as happy indoors as living on the run.
Versatile, reliable, there are few with moods so pure,
Gentle as a rainbow, waiting at your door.
And when she exercises there is no pumping iron,
Though where she ever gets to is your guess, as good as
    mine.
If every human creature could adopt her sylvan ways,
We'd live in blessed heaven for the remnant of our days.

Feline

Unperturbed in sleep, enamelling our dreams with her sheen;
Elongation and withdrawal, cushioned and cosseted,
Wantonly warm.
One breath sweeter than our poor strain –
One stroke softer than gentle wine.
Where does this luxury end? How does this cradle pretend
To circumscribe what she imbibes?

Ambition

Vacant in the living space I stand and freely stare,
Upon the fields in evening sun, upon the meadows
there.
I yearn for my heart's gladdening, for open aisles and
wood,
For glass that hints of opulence, and steel and pine and
racks of wine –
All things that promise good.
I watch the men enlist my plan, my mind into a dream,
Promising to capture land, so profligate the scheme.
Without constraint the marble floor, the subtle
marquetry,
The polished cabinets and shelves, all speak of luxury.
And angular and all awry the scaffold rakes the sky,
While there inside the honoured mind creates its
symmetry.
The fields look gentle in the sun, the last of summer's
wine;
The hill climbs steeply to the wood where darkness
sleeps awhile.
Alone with high ambition, sad company I keep;
The men are now departed – I stand and freely weep.

Nations

We seek a flag to adhere to,
For bravery or reward,
A pennant for faith and renewal,
A cross instead of a sword.
The identity strengthened or counterfeit
Anticipates every call
While nationhood finds itself burdened,
Notorious since its fall.
Is there a flag to die for,
A nation under the sun,
A people unscathed or spirited?
Perhaps there is just one.
That of the unseen general,
The master of every plan,
With a mission to shape our destiny,
Yes there is but one.

Imagination

When we're lost in fantasy, or setting words to song,
When the vague acquaintance features loud amid the
    throng;
Even memory with all its subtlety and flair
Fashions something vital in the warmth of evening air.
When we sit and muse awhile upon the haunts of spring,
When cool night breeze awakens dreams of cosmic
    reckoning;
Even psyche with its grace, invested but not earned,
Sees a solid beauty there that sense cannot disturb.
When we incubate a plan, advance from day to day,
When the elements are there to figure what we say;
Then the mind is its own realm; it stores, it makes, it
    feels,
Imagining all things; turning parchment into steel.

Ordonnance

All from a single breath,
The range and depth of all that is,
Leapt with a purpose to create
Unfathomed worlds within our human state.

And birds for every season,
Uplifted high in flight,
Bonded for the reason,
Impending in the night,
Stoop and settle and take their rest
In that unattended, promontory nest.

And the fish as now they glide,
Flickering flecks of gold, burgeoning bright,
Change their pattern with a whim, it seems,
And that reflection turns as in a dream.

So as we try to comprehend, dispute,
The strangeness of a place
Where friends are sent their enemies to contend,
And lameness limps and decadence extends –
Dream of birds and beasts and trees and men;
Await with Milton, darkly in his bliss,
The dawn of every "individual kiss".

Spring

Careless lives are prone awaiting spring,
Calls perform the rituals 'round their heads
While days are muffled, stifled in their beds.
Along the length of branches buds are set,
Witness to the fluid, oozing wet,
Breaking at the seams in tender blains of deepest red.
Growth is imminent in all affairs,
It ambushes our languid mind and powers,
Lurches to the upright from the dead.
And should the days grow long and we forget,
Remiss, unoccupied and failing yet,
Let us make impromptu moves at life,
Resurrect what seems too indolent;
Discard our winter robes
And put on painful flesh.

Ruthless

A dual love its vows exclaim
Beneath the bows and tender rain,
While ivy with a python's skin
Strangles every strength within,
And obstacles find weakness there
To intercept and strip life bare.

The welcome tree it grows opposed
By consequential ranks of foes;
But when those two in winter rain
Turn homeward with their thoughts again
The mistletoe, dear host, still grows
From cravings or desires below.

So many, so few

Standing by to count the years;
Quiet streams of believers, roads wide with regret,
Places where the few are walking,
Who we've seen or who we've met.

We ourselves are moments shining
From some casement in the night,
Strangers find the way in passing,
Through the unsuspecting light.

Well we see the ancients fighting,
Mirrored by the frigid moon,
Soon the history books are telling
What was done to what, to whom.

But the faces there are wanting,
Some sweet force is lost to us,
For we only see the corpses
Of a mystery-laden past.

Time is still when we are watching
From the outpost of our lives
Those we've loved, quite unencumbered,
By the multitude above.

When the hosts aspire to meet us
If a heavenly home we're shown,
There the earthly greeting alters:
So many to see, so few we've known.

Seagull in the City

Unguarded, unguided, unheralded bird,
Dweller in the far unknown;
Mariner without a home.
What did you dream when the tide unchained,
Coupled energy decayed,
Every fission in the soil,
All the radiant, sentient sea,
Broken in its depths – your sea?

Safe with us will be your rest,
Where the sunlight steeps the west,
Where the starlings roost by night,
Where those guests can be your guide.

Grieving for your place to see,
Mournful waves come back to me –
Black and turgid, foaming white,
Moonlit waters dead by night.

Will your seagull hosts appear?
Will they trace our homely shore?
Will our city be their stay?
For respect of you we'll wait:
Far from sea-spent wilderness
Or the foul breath of progress.

The need to rest

He was an upright, lonely man,
Spending every precious hour – asleep,
Or rather, needing every moment to forget
The torment of a life in bed.
But there is no escape – they stand him up for clothes,
He lapses back.
Quiet as a lamb he gently stands;
Impassiveness belies an agony inside,
And every face reflects his costly life.

Days cannot be counted, minutes less -
Lifetimes last eternities at rest.
Sweat soaks the unkempt bed,
And bathing is forgotten in the sweet smell of neglect.

Such a life - why has this good man seen,
Consigned to nothing, but to suffering?

For lack of love *we* have consigned him there –
For, look, we fight and, look, we don't care.

The other side of the coin

It drops and makes our fate secure,
No jealous look at what's before -
Accept serenely that which dealt
The hammer blow to fame or wealth.
Then what would fame explain to those
Whose precepts wither like the rose,
Whose colour suits the current ways,
Who call the coin before it's played?

Then instead a die is cast,
Appealing to our heart at last –
So we hasten to accept
A fragment of our future sent;
A piece of choice; a piece of art,
Expressly promised from the start –
And whatever pledge we make,
Never let our mind forsake
The nature of our gift or chance,
The fatal or renewing dart
Thrown by ages at the heart.
Conflicting messages we gain;
Reviving fortunes; causing pain.

Peace

Peace can possess without a house,
Without addition, child or spouse;
For we can inward people be,
Whose solitude is silent rest
(though inner beat is inner stress).
So garner peace like precious dew,
So swift descending, meant for you.
So light its touch on open ground,
On desert plains like manna found.
In the depth of crowded times
The wealthy prize is peace of mind;
A quiet walk, a sunrise dawn,
A brook that runs through fields unmown.
Finding times and talents press,
Seasons, clocks and rules regress –
Make yourself a lasting home;
For peace is all we have or own.

The Youth Orchestra

Passion is indulgent in the youthful years;
It bursts from adolescence
And turns with mild applause.
With melting strings and striking brass
The orchestra unfolds;
A drama in the parish church,
A teenage demiurge.
Delicate white fingers swathe a glassy tune,
While drums beat down the characters;
Emerge from monochrome.
For music shines its colours;
A fantasy, a show, a cymbal-full of ecstasy,
A lull to close.
Beneath the exposition, the festival, the verve,
Encounter there that passion
Silencing the word;
See its vital talent, our sensitive youth,
The novel generation,
Enchanting and aloof.

The Repository

What a place to lie in stony state,
Where the genes uncluttered wait for breath,
Wait for animation in their carnal nest.
What motherhood is this that dotes on blood,
What mastery of motherhood to fasten flesh,
To covet genius in an idle bed?
Memories are stored in trophied vials,
From scientists imagining mankind;
All manner of rare things will be revealed,
When infants from the darkness break their seals.
I am the mistress of repository,
Many transformations I recall
From the maker to the world below,
Brooding over essence, set in stone,
Confined to what we are and where we grow.

This side of heaven

Much is expected of those to whom much has been
given,
But ambition drives before self-sacrifice
This side of heaven.
Few are the chosen who endure for many their ransom;
And few are the kings whose battles are fought for
salvation.

Shrouds have no pockets

The glass shines perfectly tonight,
Eloquent gleams from a dresser of charms
Settled with dust, a subtle harm.

See the coins; open the globe of desires,
From ancient to modern, Roman to Tyre,
Maundy to glistening crowns.

From the wardrobe, gently coax the silk ties,
And be reminded of their deep provenance.
Then savour the sweet, rich meat and Malmsey wine –

Better to eat and drink and bide your time
Than search your treasures for solace –
For one thing is certain: your shroud will have no
    pockets.

For those that care for others

Giving without thought of reward,
For love the waiting brief;
Hanging on every word
The lover silently grieves.
Parting would ask too much,
Staying has manifest claims;
Caring will ever be such,
While tenderness remains.
Open the half-closed mind,
Entice the words from a mouth,
Patience is ever kind
When hour follows day follows month.

Worldly Wise

"And what's your excuse for failing like that?
Surely you don't have knowledge."
With impunity Worldly Wise always looks for a profit.
And that's the way the world spells the name,
Not a rarefied bone in the body;
The easy abuse of words with charm
Is a trait, is a trick that's been borrowed.
Below common sense, the spurious sense
Is the one that looks for a loser,
So instead of a garland for doing your best,
The innocent game is over.
"And don't you know why the world says that,
You fool looking ever so nervous? –
We suffer you only to make use of you son,
Are you a boy or a man with a purpose?"

Destiny

Who knows the guided mission of our souls -
When nerves transmit and molecules control?
The future flows but first its leaves are dry
Till winter wraps their message in its guise.
See then the scudding clouds of spring beyond
Above the hills whose undulance streams on;
They scour the land and dapple valley towns,
As there we sit, whose destiny seems bound.
We oversee the ranges of the land
Where sunlight gives an inkling of a plan,
But though we stay and think, we barely grow –
Who knows the guided mission of our souls?

Holidays, home or away

Tasting distant lands reverberates in spring,
When searchers seek to cleanse their souls
From winter's telling scourge,
And crocuses and daffodils address themselves in rows.
So delicate the coloured show that nature dares to bring,
So early does the optimist see summer on the wing.
The creatures take their holidays at some such time as ours
And tentative they're freed again from stifling hibernation,
While sunshine guides the tourist race with mighty jubilation.
The holidays are here for all – but then there is the packing,
The driving and the traffic, and the peace that seems so lacking.
Our papers have to be exact, and then there are the passports;
Fresh air we want, and different climes, not overcrowded airports.
So finding us abroad at last, we're feeling pretty jaundiced;
The only place we'd love to be is somewhere that is safest.
And that's not always Greece or Spain, not even Costa Brava,
For once we're home adventure's gone, but here we feel looked after!

Star of the sea

The sea can be for pleasure, as we cast our nets ashore;
The ocean gives its bounty as it never has before.
Far beyond our depth a silent pasture grows,
Where beasts and creatures replicate their patterns as
their own.
The sea can be for pleasure as we row our boats ashore,
As we push our little rafts on the cool water's floor.
The sinking sand, soft-treading joy; fevered sunshine
from above –
Our shadows dancing gaily below the Star of the Sea of
Love.
And she won't rest till she has saved all farers who she's
found,
For surely it's no pastime when hell is ocean-bound.

Youth and Age

Always looking to the future or thinking here and now,
Seeking how to beat the world when dreams began to grow.

That was then, but here we are many miles along the track
And thoughts have turned from passion-led to paltry passion-spent.

Now the future seems so small, doubts ever line that track,
Our nights repair those damaged days – regrets look ever back.

To fast or to eat

There is a simple tale to tell; to nourish or to die,
And eating takes the edge off life, while fasting tells the lie –
That without food we turn to good, and without meat we shine,
But all the time our appetite is lodged within the mind.
Perhaps a healthy hunger accentuates our taste,
And every morsel craved for prevents a carnal waste.
Though if we find our sharpened sense rails against the weak,
Just beware the war we make when we are cloaked in peace.

Tempest

The tempest fumes the wrath of gods on ancient soil and
mythical seas;
The exploits of the great and good are infinitesimal to
these.
Twisters pinion-swirl the plains and snatch the very
Earth's domain,
While surging floods can tear our towns and cast in mud
once florid ground.

And in the garden peacefully, or where the children play,
Another passage keeps its course, far out of fierce harm's
way.
Chequered lives, shuddering souls and fallen strays go on
to glory,
For with the tempest comes the swell,
When anger's lost its fury.

The Map etc.

That's not how it is on the map.
I imagined a place full of sweet suggestions;
Mellow light on stone walls, flowers on the corners,
Church bells echoing still and grand steeples.
Not the noise of cars full of outsiders fuming at the lights,
Shopfronts boarded up in part and alleys with their broken glass.
This can't be the postcard traded town,
Once thought of far away, in the east.
But this is where we dwell, and where we toil;
Not where art's imagination passes.

Then go from here far south by routes unknown,
Ponder in the map your mountain home;
No contour lines prepare us for the sight of majestic peaks
And sunlight dipping white, down silver-twisting valleys,
So far below to be dreamlike.
No road is ever drawn like this; to taste the danger,
To see the abyss.
Take the map and nature: nature's won.
The map excites, but can't compare,
Unless it makes our forlorn towns seem fair.

Frustration

So many awkward knots to untie,
A thousand songs that are dumb;
Fumble and try to be heard, to be seen,
And another strange day is undone.

Day upon day, we enter the night,
Intrepid, to sit in the quiet,
And wage with our thoughts a war upon Earth
For the new ones now given birth.

For all the chaos now understood,
For all the friends by the bed,
We thank the power that promises good
And turns despair into rest.

Liberty

Well we think of distant skies
And knowledge left at home.
Dust cannot ideas mar,
Nor shadows light enthrone.

Well we find the ripened fruit,
The colours brighter by far
Than any sight to be revealed,
Than any accessible art.

Well we reach and touch our goal,
Liberty drawn from clay;
In the night-time darkness roams
Around perpetual day.

Remembrance

Childhood voices, raised once, falling as rain,
Lining the straight, shouting for her, calling her name.
Onward she speeds, flashing delight;
A father to love, a father with pride –
Over the finishing line.
Never forget that poignant vignette,
A relic alive, condensing a life.
And energy coursing through youth of our dreams,
When visions they race in the heat of our brains –
Past all contenders, furious to win,
Desire and exhaustion, running through pain.
Perhaps we could run as once we ran then,
Or stand aside to see winning again:
If we could sprint and catch our careless youth
We would recall that hope, that joy, that truth.

Flux

Look upon the water, flourishing and bright, taking
essence from its flight, pouring down from dark
regions, cascading into light, or with ice afloat shifting
when it breaks, at its appointed time, its particular
place –
Where the waterfall wakes.
Only flux and flow free the vital chain from stagnant
pool,
Just as out of nothingness our blood and mortal coil.

The sea unfurls its grey and blue and throws upon the
shore dead things, spent lives, husks and bones,
moving nevermore.
The fire opens tongues, to lick the distant sky, but
nurtured in those caverns deep it trembles where they
lie –
Those ancestral ones that knew what is found today,
Traces of the message left when lifetimes drift away.

The Blackwater

The Danes haunt the estuarine shore –
The muddied waters lap; no anger roars.
Underneath a clouded, pale-faced sky,
Silence is the final gull-swept remedy.

Relics are the memories gone before;
Fright the visage floating under;
Pearls the colour of this shore
When light persuades surrender.

And the English, Saxon king,
Now in bronze above; like a victor,
Once a slave – a warrior or a wretch we say;
A hero for the town, or killer in his day.

Puzzles, Problems and Mysteries

What do we gain from a puzzle?
What do we find in a quiz?
Not much more than we had at the first;
Perhaps a reply at best.

How do we handle a problem?
How do we tackle that test?
With not much more than solutions,
Unravel the answer and put it to rest.

But then we discover a mystery,
A strange, unlikely place;
A person we know, but not quite enough;
A character held on trust.

The mystery lies deep, wherever it's seen;
Beneath the cover of dawn,
Or down at the nightfall where silence retains
The breath from the silvery moon.

A Symbol

You are the messenger of power,
Idling never, always gripped with strength,
Pert with desire and shaped with expense -
Waiting for release through the byways of joy
Or passages of death.
You are a badge of concept, proudly intent;
A lock for the key, as you summon the force
To travel your road, to pursue or to flee.
The road is your master, it bids you be gone,
To search for a reason, a blood-brother bond.
And there in the distance you waver then roar,
You clench with the steel, embrace with the impact,
Softly reveal your pride and your purpose,
The dangerous thrill of meeting your partner –
The half that you kill.
For you are the metal that shed its attire,
You are the message that found its desire.

The Outsider

On, about, around,
The ball and the hunters play the winter's ground.
Flying with possession, trampling on the wing,
In and out with nimble feet,
About, around and on -
The watchman casts a wary eye
On strangers that are gone.

Futile seems the chase,
The prey disperses and appears,
Into flurries in the mind,
Into young men's fears.

And the sparse crowd cheers,
And the dull tackles thud,
And the expletives far away,
Muted over playing fields,
On his memorial day.

He is the keeper of the gate,
He handles on his own,
Directing from the platform of long ago.
And when the trial and test is won,
Commanding his own land,
Outsider into hero leaps –
But still a lonely man.

God blew and they were scattered

The mighty vessels, empty souls, searching vainly for a
raid;
An offshore assault with not an enemy engaged.
When all was risked and all was lost beyond the shores to
be besieged,
Those wheeling birds looked on with mirth upon the
rugged seas.

Only rampant England could conjure such a day,
With old marauding skies and powers along the way.
A victory so marvellous, without a thrust or blow,
Became a shining legend struck, when God stood here
below.

Ugliness

There is a blight that blackens the leaves of the once-
pruned tree,
A curling parasitic curse that's blown on high in the
song-filled sky.
But with new, fair shoots unfolding, never to be undone,
They surge ahead with hope, they love the matchless sun.

Disease hangs ugly and alone in the peaceful air,
But with evening's touch, deep, rich red blooms intense
with ghostly green, where nothing seems to ail, and
nothing cruel is seen.

Our blight cripples the bones; whether we're uncovered
by the sun
Or shivering in the rain, there's no rich soil that soaks
our veins,
No restoration for our plagues - only the blood that clots,
And the dirt that's lifted for an early grave.

The idea of currency

Daisies don't appear in towers or concrete squares, they gently sway to breeze, making us eager to go where they belong or where they look, with yellow face each one – the sun!
Our creatures don't appear in crowded streets, they nestle in the country far from town and find association in the field, their concourse in the balmy air.

We, entranced, forget the natural ways; we televise the rain, the wetness of the grass, the passage of the stars - inside; and then that unremitting language of our time, the economic tale, the fiscal compromise.
What of information not disclosed, ideas not explained, what of hunger we can't share and danger that we sense, yet unaware?

There was a pageant that retraced our past, with little boats against the river squall, and precious boats with monarchy aboard. Some saw empire in this reign, for what it's worth; a time of enterprise and wealth; a time when ideas were currency and more –
Now that currency seems the only idea.

Foolishness

Foolishness, conceit and wisdom,
You'd think there'd be some change,
But everywhere we look we find these synonyms remain.
For very little knowledge distinguishes the wise
And those conceited cynics all people they despise.
Perhaps the so-called fools are best,
Knowing little of the world,
For all the good should love them,
And their story's seldom heard.

Respectability

What a bore to be respectable,
To be always trimmed and kept;
Perhaps I'll be respectable
When I'm truly dead.
For then they'll say, to speak no ill,
'He rose to trials sent',
If only to acknowledge
A life that seemed well meant.

To kiss

They were embattled by many troubles
When in youth they were driven to kiss,
And what depth and what fire
Conjoined such couples with a wasting desire.
Heat quickens the blood in a rapturous grasp
As moist and feeble turns to feverish clasp;
And every exchange is coiled like this,
To push and search for the fabled kiss.
And they were young those passions and friends,
Lovers and seekers compelled to the end;
With some desperation they muffled that shout,
Seeking that strange destination, a mouth.

Great aunt we kiss her once on the cheek,
Gently our mother kisses our neck;
See how the family summons this type,
See how the tenderness touches so light –
Nowhere the bruising battle so rough
Played out in secret struggles of love.
Sometimes a foreigner kisses us twice,
Or then a husband kisses a wife;
The ritual ends with that touch so light,
Once on the forehead to seal a life.

Happenings

When the time is still and cold and rare,
And rooks upon the ruined walls appear,
Then the deepening darkness makes its way,
And the evening's shrill exchange edges departed day.
This is not a place of rest, far less a place observed,
And no, the passages of age seem neither new nor old.
But there's an untold story here, or film without its
    words,
Replaying for the characters long dead within these walls.
The endless hours and endless wars are now reduced to
    this –
An imprint in obscurity that reason can't resist.
The prison made by winter, the northern wind and rain,
Once held a timid captive of fortune, might and fame.
Now leave that cast of dead men to dwell upon their
    deeds,
That spawned the swell of haunting and sowed eternal
    seeds:
Extract from darkness some pure light when you are
    warm in bed,
And hope for things of honeyed south, with tropical
    intent.

Vocations

Lighten the load of vocation to save a place for the young,
Those roamers and rollers whose fervour is spent on idols that gravitate fun.
They too have a wire to tread as they rock with unsteady feet,
And they fall just as holy ones did from the vessel into the deep.
Whenever the wars have opened the wounds of young and old alike,
The old that were young, and young never old are common souls in the fight.
Count and score the winnings on the path we tread,
And triumph will be spoiled, as war negates the best.
But this can be vocation, to be shed with blood on the ground;
A kind of repatriation, a gracious memory found.
Then a higher calling, in life at such a cost, in death imparts new fortune
To those we thought were lost.

Medals

Your medals are silent, they haven't spoken yet;
They don't display the action that once was spent;
They don't convey the hurt, the anger or regret,
The violence felt with grim intent.

So what can they embody, these medals on the chest?
An armoury of bravery, a token while you rest.
They do say you fought for right
And fought to free the slave -
Please show the map upon your face,
For always colours fade.

Christmas

Ask the cherubs as they play,
Or powers and dominions in a row
If Christmas with the stable, ox and hay
Will visit us at home in town today -
And they say gaily, 'not quite as yesterday'.
But still the season sends its gifts and candlelight,
Not starlight seen before,
But gathering gleams of childhood play
And scattered toys in bright array.
When the child smiles on Christmas Day,
Where is sadness but to wish it stay?
For joy and sadness are not far away.

White

The marbles were cleaned for purity,
Those that faced the Grecian sun;
Though paint covered their whiteness
When the world of art was young.

An imperial madness found virtue in stone,
And raised a monstrous race –
Of figures lining a field of dreams
With an inhuman cast of the face.

Then his soaring obelisk,
Raised unspeakably high
Boasts with a clinical paleness
That still offends the eye.

The studies in white are framed for the just,
Eccentric but filling the room,
With attitude, tenderness, faces that haunt,
And brush strokes whose nothing is known.

There is no message the blank page can write,
No quarry that finds us a stone,
Whose grandeur matches the craftsman's power,
As long as the power is his own.

No tyrant can nullify innocence,
With colour, shape or excess -
But now we're the modern day movers,
And our virgin girls dress in red.

Roman summers

Chariots rattle in the dusty summer,
Scrubland features, dearth of rain.
When rain comes glamour suffers,
And where blood fell the dogs now roam.

This is our southern summer,
Where they shed their scattered fame.
The land is all ochre and lustre
And its heart is hard without rain.

The dustbowl of Rome shelters its pain
Deep within sand and stone.
The sun in rising flatters its shame,
And where blood fell the dogs now roam.

When time will waste

The lineaments of time are tracing shadows on a face,
Which moving play the clouds' own tune,
Which all too soon will cease.
And every structure that we shape,
Or edifice construct
Implodes with resonation on the day
When time itself will waste.

Journeying

The children move in time along the beach,
Hand in hand along the reach of bay –
Equidistant from the sea and shore,
They tread the sequined sands.
Fair hair and blue chemise and lifted eyes
They march with alabaster hands.

They move ahead as they had gone before,
Footsteps marking softly where they tread;
Untroubled by the distant ocean's roar –
Towards the misty church on chalk-white hill;
Lonely waiting for their look to dwell;
Lonely calling for their ears its bell.

Missing friends

Why do our friends desert us today?
Is it the beleaguering wind
That lifts the leaves of the Judas tree
And rolls the ripe, red apples on the branch
That leads them from harm?
Do they secretly devour the seeds in their discreet pods,
While they endure the storm?
Shuttered in our room, we seek the company of birds –
But they are gone;
Not even a rook calls, or a dove makes song.

Night's awakening

The window blind, pale and thin and frayed
Waves in the night's cool awakening,
And floral, pastel shapes upon the wall
Are darkened, and their colour chastened.

It is that dangerous time when day's clarity is lost
And stars through inky nights are shot.

Far out over the whistling fields a dog cries;
A plaintive sound – from which home does it rise?
Or is the creature lost to man's poor care,
And does it suffer in night's thoroughfare?

Violence

The hatred that breeds violence and revenge
Cowers before the judgment it exacts.
While grief and pain from anguish can be cleansed,
The punishment for torture wrings its hands.

Hunted

The wood blooms heavy in its own decay,
And through the airlocked trees
And sticky, stubborn leaves
Gaunt November radiates its icy ray;
And mournful, slanting, fledgling sun
Brushes the trickling day.

Creatures rise with instinct for their eyes,
Examine tracks, scrutinise the air
Sensing infiltration in their lairs.
Their quickness labours in an earthy clutch;
Entrails quiver liquid-thin with grim disease
And autumn's stony touch.

Above a morbid pool the mist gathers its breath
Where the deer stands silent,
Sweating a shroud of death.
Within the close and fettered land
A valley filled to ripeness wastes around,
And wily foxes incubate the thrill of muted, bugle sighs
And distant, querulous hounds.

The lord adeptly mounts the stallion of the breed;
Around him grooms with garlands wait,
Meticulous in gold and red and green.
Knots are fastened, torsion-tied with ease,
Leather straps hang sensitive to noble feet,

Caparisons are matched and showered with gorgeous
  thread,
And jewels glisten gaily in their velvet bed.
Then cobbles crack to the horses' tread;
Carried on the wing to utter joy;
Conveyed by birds on high to augur dread.

Underneath her coverlet the lady takes her rest;
Mystifying dreams play round her head;
Pale crêpes winnow softly on her chalk-white hands,
Drifting in and out of sleep while stratagems are planned.

And when the rocks and cliffs rebound with strife,
An undeciphered panic strikes the victim's heart;
Tearing untoward for higher ground,
It grinds towards its fall –
For all around the skilful foil prevents escape;
And blood in droplets
          gutters on the green
And crush of crimson
          seals its vital fate.

A Continental Plate

Who can defend the opaque mêlée deep?
What can entice like a matrix net?
Rocking and lurching, denying sleep;
And the awful groan of rope thread.

They're racked above to a ravening crew,
Staring, sidelong, ghostly –
Leaking to the inky blue.
Great grey fish pout and writhe,
Langoustines dance with bursting eyes.
From cells like cellulose they shine.

An elemental shock commands their fate
And then a party's set –
For the continental china plate.

Triptych

You remind me all too well, with understated smile,
And boundless features of a face so mild.
With brown enrobed and crown of stippled gold,
Your eyes engage a space, from their homely throne.

And symmetry resides quite simply in those eyes.

They understand the manner of the plan;
Endurance marked for all, on finely folded hands.
And, for us, you explicate the text;
Your reach, unstretched, protects the nameless word;
And, fastened gently until death,
You annunciate our fate, unread.

Beside you, staying cloak and touching stem,
Your mother and our mother rests
In tender greeting sat expressed;
The glow of expectation quietly kept,
The charge accepted with a trust impressed.

Eclipsing cold vermilion in the garden of regret.

Then, close, the posture of your sister saint,
Draped in pastel shades and cracks of ancient paint;
With studied clasp of book and branch;
The lilies that she chose, the book encased;
A bud so timely closed.

A three-sided equation

Triangles of the ancient east
        Triangles of shining glass
Triangles that rule the heart

What holds the key to unlock such design
Which is willing us still within the mind?
The strength and the failure;
Confinement and release;
Is it all held together?
Is it all of a piece?

Belonging

Walking by the sea's shore, I held a stone;
Whole as a mountain, full as a throne.
Its place of belonging was robbed by my hand;
Its place was becoming before it was found.

Once we too were enshrined by another;
Once we were held by the walls of a mother.
But then we were taken and offered a place;
Then we were called by a name and by grace.

The Grand Marquee

Clattering, chattering, tinselling talk,
Merging in eddies across the lawns –
Laughter of winning, sparkling with rosé;
Hot competition for trivia folk.

We languish in the shadows,
Clutch at benches, catching flowers;
Searching for solace beneath the branches.
Charged with emotion we quicken to action,
Drawn by the shimmering tent –
Heavenly attraction.

Perfect shade within, and invitations won,
We trail through coolness to our seats,
To sample simple fun.
New wine flows from hand to hand,
But paupered we sit (turmoil to think),
Sensing the scent of a strange land;
A party in the great outdoors,
Where (disallowed) we drink.

A Village Tree

The wry tumult of a green embrace;
The sky's carpet spread with shade,
Exploring ground and wall and grave;
Creating grandeur from a little rain.
She's a captive, yet she's wild;
Born with the mother, growing with the child;
Gently chiding, coaxing, calming,
Bearing no harshness,
Set with a charm.
A tree with a glimmer, a gilded dream,
Simply reposing in the afternoon.
Her lowly mantle trimmed with flowers,
Just waiting for those evening hours.
And when the world has passed and gone,
She stays, and glows, and lingers on.

Maldon – beyond the promenade

Shuffling in the sandpit,
Keeping out an eye
For uncomplicated children
And their broken castle pies;
A woman asks me bluntly:
"Do you come from Wales?"
"I've seen a person like you, across the miles"
But no, I'm just a local, dreaming of the seas,
Of Ynys Môn or Innisfree,
And all those aching trees.
But there's beauty here in Maldon,
Beyond the promenade,
Through the tinkling of the tackles
And the whispers in the yards.
Just around the outpost,
Gazing from the prow,
The open sea, deliciously,
Is moaning for the town.

Swimming to the island

Freedom and isolation motivate
As I take the plunge, into the depths,
Into the clear, diamond Mediterranean,
Its hollows and coves reddish brown
Under the immovable sun.
And my skin so supple and tanned,
Glistening on one so young.
Adventure beckons for the taking
As the empty isle lies waiting,
As gently I go plashing,
Seeing the bottom sway with weed,
Away from civilization, away from need;
Ever toward the mysterious object,
Set like a brilliant continent,
Not far from reach.
Then, struggling for foothold on the rocks,
The body feels heavy and hurts,
After such experienced bliss
Of joyful weightlessness.

What I have written, I have written

Exalted, defined in just one line,
Transcendent it brands the darkened sky.
We never saw that hour's new dawn,
Nor image as the veil was torn:
But testament we have and text,
And suffering soul and sacred head.
We asked for mighty words to change -
But they stay;
We looked for triumph in the sky -
And there it is in just one line.

Release

There, He told you, that's the lot;
Facts are sorted, drawn the dots.
The image quickens on the page,
The captive slips off mighty chains.
The tomb is empty, work is done;
The sky stands startled,
Flocks are dumb.
The engine falters, never to regain
Its impetus, its thrust again.
The heart is open, joy abounds;
Don't let us lose what now we've found.

Peace again

The Lord is our guide
And with Him we reside,
Until the moor is green again,
Until the shore lies quiet again,
Until the noon remains with morning
And the dawn breaks clear from men.
A place where love alights again,
Without the dulling tears of rain.
Until the piano tunes unfaded
Play with drifting chords unaided;
And gaiety has grace again.

The remit

The remit keeps us strong
And brings the past along.
A quiet, lonely day
Enlivened by your eye;
The truth is sunk and set
Beyond the edge of sky.
The sun declares your worth,
The shadow tracks our path.
Within the realm of day
All sadness ebbs away.

Float in the heavens

Float in the heavens
The birds of the sky;
Under your measure
All husbandry's dry.
The nestlings are hatching
The root of the plan,
And all before us
Is stretched by your hand.

At the last

I long for a day that is fuller,
A night that is darker, or brighter with stars,
A happiness more joyful,
A hope more powerful, after waiting is past.

I want experience that is deeper,
A taste that is sweeter,
A reality clearer,
A touch that is shared.

Then will I love with a sated desire,
Then will I know what will always be clear,
And through simplicity, sanctity there,
Such will be answers to longings and prayer.

* 9 7 8 1 7 8 0 3 5 6 3 5 8 *

ND - #0194 - 060826 - C0 - 197/132/8 - PB - 9781780356358 - Matt Lamination